SAGACITY

POEMS

LAURIAN TALER

GONG PUBLISHING
TORONTO

Sagacity

By the same author:

Almost Essentials
On a Blade of Grass
Under the Blue Sky
L.A.U.G.H. (e-book)

SAGACITY
POEMS

GONG PUBLISHING
TORONTO

www.gongnog.com

ISBN 978-1-926477-01-5

DEDICATION

To all
lovers of wisdom
for themselves
and mostly for others

PREFACE

We all strive for something. In our quests we receive, through the street or the family, the school or the experience, the mistakes and the random acts of life, a certain capacity to affirm the presence of doses of intelligence that we might confound with wisdom.

It is a given that wisdom comes late, if ever, in someone's life. As such, we all assume that it must be associated with old age. It is not for me to claim that wisdom may not be encountered with youth, but for them there is mostly a recognized mental brilliance whose values have other depths and weight than in what is attributed to the sages of old. Wisdom, or sagacity, implies a condensed, filtered and reworked intelligence, expressed sometimes in short, powerful sentences, but mostly in the proper decisions to act according to certain circumstances in order to obtain the right results.

Knowledge, understanding, disposition, control, judgement, action- all come into play to lead the wise ones towards a beneficial goal. Or to suggest to others what path to choose.

My "Sagacity" is just a title to a collection of poems written late in life, when life's burdens have seemed to become lighter. Although I was a nationally published poet at 11, I lost my initial "production" in the labyrinth of too many activities. Once retired and focussed on writing songs, I became aware that some of my lyrics were sometimes, what else, well, lyrical. This is why I have chosen some of these lyrics, which are incorporated in three other volumes of lyrics only, to be introduced among creations that asked to be put down on paper as poetry.

But still, why this title? Could it have anything to do with the present that my father gave me for my Bar-Mitzvah, a book about Spinoza? Of course, I hardly understood anything from it at that time, except for the fact that my father kept the philosopher in high esteem. Sure, I always had a tendency for contemplation, but it was only when I have learned more about nature and the systems theory that I came upon the impression that I might have understood a bit of what is going on in the many little worlds that we come across sometimes. Of these worlds, the one that we humans inhabit attracted my interest in a peculiar way. It is with this in mind that I have tried, both in song and lyrics, in poetry and other writings, to capture and describe my and others' sentiments and relationships as forms of wisdom or lack of it. Going through the titles of some poems, I noticed a number of them having something to do with sages. That's how I come about the title of this collection. Maybe I wasn't wise enough to do such a thing, but then, what the heck, lots of writers and philosophers have made their blunders. Why not me?

You may find that I have embraced mostly a traditionalist style in poetry writing. That is due in good measure to the fact that I grew up with rhyming cadenced songs, learned from my sister Viorica, seven years my senior and my main caretaker when mother was busy making a living in the absence of my father, who was wrongfully taken as a forced labourer and war prisoner for over four years during and after the Second World War.

I do use free verse as rarely as I can, especially when I need to translate. Apart from that, my ideas about free versification come counter to the fact that I disdain notions of limitlessness, like absolute freedom, which to me appears as a clear impossibility. Then there is the aspect of dullness and lack of coherence given by extensive jumps in thinking when reading free verse, which I again try to avoid.

This is why I stand against what I wrongfully thought was my word invention, prosetry, in my view a prose that pretends itself to be poetry. Maybe the prosets would all jump up against me, but somebody has to call a spade a tool.

Some poems in this volume have been translated from originals written by me either in Romanian or in French.

Laurian Taler

Toronto, October 2014

TABLE OF CONTENTS

THE SAGE 1

The crazier we are
The more we laugh
Proclaimed the sage
And then started to cry
You see, he had difficulty
To act crazy
Because his mentality
Too cautious, too circumspect,
Too restricted and too abstemious
Full of respect, full of virtue

Too moderate,
Always careful
And hindered,
But without sin
He carried his moderation
Good mannered in soap-bubble
To the extreme.

That's why he's still crying
On the outside
But who knows
What is
In his intimate inside

THE SAGE 2

The crazier we are
The more we laugh
Said the sage and then
So as not to miss it,
He started to laugh
You see, what a pity
Our sage, at his age
Was a madman.

His wisdom,
Of thinking too hard
Has affected him so much
That he became obsessed
To acquire laughter
He became obsessed
All of a sudden to be mad

-It is crazy to be alive
Without laughing, better to die
Because of a laugh
The madman used to say
As not to contradict himself
He started to laugh
And to maintain himself laughing
Always, day and night,
He kept on doing crazy things

The crazier, the merrier
And more we laugh,
The crazier we are

Crazy sage, you were,
Because your laughter,
To contradict yourself,
The damned sage.

THE THREE MOST SAGE

My philosophy teacher
With a boxer's feature
Son of an Orthodox priest
And in lectures grand artist
In his way trying to flatter
And to pull my leg much better
One day told me a true joke
That my ancient blood evoke.

"Can you say on just one page
Who were world's the three most sage?"
As I said no, he said, "Pity,
It's no joke, and it is witty,
Good to know is for a Jew
Where from your talents grew.
First of sages, Jew as well,
Said, of spirit we all dwell,
So the world believed him God,
Messiah who walked on sod.
Second sage, he full of rage,
Kind of Jewish, not to smatter,
Said and wrote, all is in matter,
And to make things dreary
Launched the surplus theory,
Wait, the third sage was a stone,
Of course, Jewish to the bone,
All the world he mesmerized
'Cause he matter energized
And in short time, pace to pace,
He connected time to space
So, he being sensitive,
Said loud,
All is relative."

WHO LOSES HIS CHILDISH HEAD

Who loses his childish head
Loses his head
Says an old saying,
I am restless
I don't know
Who found it
And what will then he do
With a poet's head
Who loses his childish head
Remains with the neck
At the end
I 'm uneasy
'Cause the neck, at my age
Is full of rage
Yes, my neck is furious
It has the fury to write
Doesn't read well at sight
Has no mouth to excite
My neck is straight, all straight,
But to left it is turned as of late
The ink is bloodily flowing
From my neck and I don't know
What did I really lose,
The head, the childhood,
The youth use,
The confidence
Or simply put, the conscience.

PRESENT

For the pleasure of your encounter
For the pleasure of looking at you
For the pleasure of talking, touching, caressing you
For the pleasure of understanding you
For the pleasure of seducing you
For the pleasure of making you enjoy
For the pleasure of having let you go
For the pleasure of forgetting you
For the pleasure of finding you again
For the pleasure of regaining you
For the pleasure of having loved you
And loving you again and again and again
For the pleasure of sharing with you
The hopes and the despairs
The white days and the black ones
For the pleasure of waiting together
The arrival of our children
For the pleasure of seeing them grow
As flowers and fruits of our love
For the pleasure of always seeing them
With their bright looks and their happy smiles
For the pleasure of knowing them
And of making them know the world
For the pleasure of our joys
That from time to time flood us over
For the pleasure of your ecstasies
And your cuddles and my ecstasies
For the pleasure of having united
Your good, soft soul to my crazy one
I give you the only diamond
Of your lover, of your spouse,
My life

THE PASSING

The river extends its body
Towards the eager sea
Caressing the harbour.
The quay remains empty,
Sails are not in view,
The sky is low
The silence tortures
My aches, that sing
The leaking of an earth
Into the huge sea
The passing of my matter,
Of my existence.

WINTER THOUGHTS

You sent us a Snowman
We so much enjoyed,
We hope's not an omen
Winter to avoid,
We might go to places
Cold bones up to warm,
You know we are aces
To circle a storm

So better prepare
A chimney so hot
We might land down there
On your home and your lot

We might bring a good jar
Of Schnapps or boiled wine,
We'll keep ready a rose far
In your mouth or in mine

A slow tango we'll dance
Our bones to protect,
We should fall in a trance
Or should stay quite erect

Winter, freezing or snow
What the weather will bring-
Our spirits not low,
We'll think always of SPRING!

0207 CHILDREN

Children,
Children are the spice of life, for
Children
Give you reasons for your hopes, for
Children
Bliss in all hearts flower
Our lives empower
Are the fruits of love

Children
We expect them for so long, as
Children
Make us always to belong, for
Children
Shape our lives with meaning
Fill our lives with feeling
Children make us strong

As we love them, in time
Their love is so sublime
They fill our hearts ahoy
With pride and joy
As we love them in time
Their love is so sublime
In life they are what we all call
Our goal.

TIME FLOWERS

My flowers were always blue
They breathed the desire for happiness
Mirrors of the huge cover
That keeps us away from absolute,
So tiny that only the babies
Could touch them with the fingers
Making them click
Icy, unhearable sounds
For the earthy ears.

My flowers were always blue
Remaining somewhere on the plains
Unseen for anybody's eyes
Melting with their tremor of petals
My time for happiness.

CHAIN

Life is a chain of decisions
Life is of blunders and visions
Life is the crossroads you pass
Life is surpassing your class

Roads are when narrow, when wide
Those that you take, you decide
Roads take you down, or uphill,
Choices are always your deal

It's what you settle to do
Whether yourself or with crew
Sometimes you try and you err
And that's when hardships occur

But if you think and decide
And from life's trials don't hide,
Happiness plenty or strife,
You will have made it your life.

WHEN WE WERE VERY YOUNG

When we were very young*
We also were among
The ones that dreamed of spots
Without haves and have-nots
But ended in between
Although we were so keen
To see and to be seen
Above you'd call the mean
When we were very young

* book by A. A. Milne

BLOODLETTING

It's time to wake up
Stretch your lazy bones
And wash the brain
Of the misty dreams
Empty green lungs of that cloacal air
That streams your tissues full of damp
It's time to let out
That bloody black thick blood
And change it with the ruby crystal broth
Long fermented in the veins of history
Put on sky some sons of the sun
And after thriving the crops of the mind
Harvest the needed serenity.

RESHAPE

Who knows what was in that colour
That made me believe in happiness
Who knows what was in those looks
That challenged the deeps of eternity
I was a handful of sand
On the side of a resting lake
And her blow reshaped me a troubadour
To sing the blaze of the souls
Trembling for each other's glance
The only harvest of life
That keeps us moving to and from.

TENSION

What she wanted from me was the language of flowers,
And light smiles and big laughs under delicate showers.
Yes, she wanted the honey of life in my eyes,
But before she could ask, timely thrown were the dice,
As my temper and gait and my tortuous ways
Hellas, cast were in flesh, in my neuron lace,
And to change I could not, as the flowers bore fruit,
And my soul gathered ash for desire, and soot.

She continued to look with the eyes of her youth,
When I sparked at her feet, my glance ready to sooth,
Whether now that her ups alternate with her downs,
I can tremor inside without showing an ounce

And am scolded that life isn't gilded no more
As if I am the only to produce the ore.
But if two are just two and they don't make a one
I have no strength to dig to uncover the sun,

When my ups are her ups and her soul is divine
She know that I'm hers and that only she's mine
Then my eyes carry flowers, my words bless her path,
But what comes aftermath, oh, what comes aftermath?

ELITISM

It's so good to think to high
It's so well to mind of sky
It's so full to feel belief
And to wonder from the cliff
It's a pleasure to meet yeses
And avoid all kind of messes
It is great to sense the scents
And to play with many friends
Without need to have to do
All the things that make skin blue
It is such a funny matter
To keep doing nothing better
That the comedy in range
Is to want the world to change

1303 WHO CAN TASTE HAPPINESS

Music & lyrics ©Laurian Taler, 2006

Who can taste happiness
With this global progress
In which you have no time
For your lover

You get emails all day
And you push text away
While your cell phone 's a buzz
Every moment

You must work twenty-four
You must work until sore
And commuting 's a bore
And takes time.

Who can taste happiness
When the planet's a mess
In which man is to man
Adversary

Who can taste happiness
If more people have less
Than to keep them alive
For a fortnight

Life's expendable for
Those who sell arms and gore
With a commerce that runs
Billions
When to flourish we could
Make peace ever, bring food
To the hungry and should
Spread the love

Sagacity

Who can taste happiness
When the planet's a mess
In which man is to man
Adversary

Who can taste happiness
If more people have less
Than to keep them alive
For a fortnight

When to flourish we could
Make peace ever, bring food
To the hungry and should
Spread the love

FROM A DREAM

You threw words at me, hot stones,
You threw hot stones made of sharp sounds
At me, and I had to catch them with my mind
And grind them into a grey paste
That had to be pushed heavily,
As it wouldn't flow alone.
You wondered why did I miss
Most of your lectures
And how will I pass your exam.
Well, I was busy, molding slowly that paste
Into my own divine comedy of errors
While your blabber was soft-landing
On your listeners' desks
In that rainbow room.
You wondered why did I wander
Away from you, brilliant catapulter
Of hot stones made of sharp sounds,
And I could only retort that my time wasn't yours
That my time and my molder were changing
The paste into hot boulders to fry
Avid minds searching for immeasurable immensity.

LIKE AN INNER SPRING

Like an inner spring, suddenly released,
A child has jumped from sleep, of her dream now pleased,
Utterly decided to change dream in fact,
Rushing into life, busy will to act
And with teeth and charm, elbowing along
Noble deeds she did, trembling limbs in song
Ode to life and people, family and man,
Adding zest to movement, as only she can
Seeing through the bodies, seeing through their time
Tilting spaces inwards, flowing in the mime
Resonating fire, shaking souls from trance
And arousing matter to enjoy its dance.

YOU ARE

You are a boat
On the river of time
You are within
A blue gondola rhyme

You are a sail
That is forcing the wave
You are a sailor
Strong winds knows to save

You are a glimpse
Of the thought in the word
You are the meaning for which
Oh so bright is the world

You are.

IT WILL COME A DAY

It will come a day
When stretched in my bed
I will plentifully feel
The joy of my death
Angels of cartoon
Will take me to that river
And give me a wash
To cover me with sins
Only so I'll have the permit
For the entrance to soap heaven
Keeping up my jeans

IT WILL COME A NIGHT

It will come a night
Like an old man's white beard
I will fly and fly around it
Not dipping a finger-nail either
Into that keratinic shining lattice.
Light flutter of arms
Will send my emotions to sleep
While body and what remains of the soul
Will continue to wander
In search of that mystery stair
To bring me down to my goal

IT WILL COME AN HOUR

It will come an hour
Split so much in minutes
Split so much in seconds
Split in such split seconds
That no tree or flower
That no bee or bower
That no brain or breather
Under such a cuss
In a split of splittings
In the crash of crashings
Will feel it ever pass

UPSIDE-DOWN WORLD

It will come a time
When roots will grow
To the yellow sky
And more than one sun
Will cool blue above us.
We'll have to dig hard
To see flowers
Hiding their shame there down
Mankind flesh will turn meat
And who'll be able to say
Why are so many stars
Squeezed under the feet?

DREAM ENOUGH

Music & lyrics ©Laurian Taler,1998

A1
Let's go back to our primal
State of innocence and mood
Let's go back to our childhood
When to wonder we still could

CHORUS
'Cause childhood is a dream
And dreams are from the soul
We cannot dream enough
To get to our goal
'Cause childhood is a dream
And dreams are from the soul
We cannot dream enough
To get to our goal

A2
Let's imagine our wonders
Let's transform them into play
And become the equal players
In a new and better way

A3
Let's curb noises into music
And turn shadows into light
Let's learn how to grow with nature
And to channel our might

A4
Let us conquer all the darkness
In the forest of mankind
Let us bring the light of loving
In the soul and in the mind

CLOSING CHORUS
'Cause childhood is a dream
'Cause childhood is a dream
'Cause childhood is a dream
And dreams are from the soul
We cannot dream enough
We cannot dream enough
We cannot dream enough
To get to our goal

WHY DO I WANT YOU

Why do I want you in my arms?

'Cause right and tender is your flesh
And charms are on it scattered
As on your bosom and your whimper?
'Cause sight you show that dreams hold still
With sublime harmonies
And which inspire deadly souls
On site to turn alive?
Or maybe it's the play of shades
That I caught without knowing,
A most profound and antic play
That asks for skies in twos
I am afraid the answer is
Not in the words that scamper
But in the flows of silent waves
Between flutters of eyelids
And in the slow hinders
Of deep and darker waters
The sadness gets in deeper
When waves are not reflected,
When waters are too clear
And do not turn from stones

I thought, again I wobble
And get imbued with shadows
When clocks are beating night time
With wings that flutter dark
But how easy I stumble
When water's crystal-clear
And however reflections
To gather I cannot

THE DISORDER

With much serenity I received
The Disorder of Canada,
Not that I deserved it most,
Considering childhood ideals
And the powers that be,
But my queen is much too far
And I need her even farther
From the beaver's pond;
Then it is the tight embrace
Of the Southern Neighbour
With its succulent sucking
Of what counts of value,
The oh, so opportune
Equality of opportunity
That makes us equal
With the moles,
A decisive separation
Of secular from security,
A perfect effect
Of religious dizziness
With entrenched, embedded
Spinners of the real
Into an intolerable,
Insufferable tolerance
To further cloud the unnatural
Flow of riches to a top
Under the unblemished emblem
Of peace, order, and
God government,
Since we, the mortals,
Equals to the moles,
Can't govern ourselves,
Un-anointed and dirty
From the burrows of Earth;

Sagacity

Not only serene I am now,
But much resplendent
With my Disorder of Canada,
That I declare here and there,
That I won't give it up
For anything but Her change.

EINSTEIN'S UNIVERSE

A philosophic stone, a rock,
The fundamental question
He knew how to dock:
- I wonder if god
In his grand game
To lay the sod
To build for himself
A Universe
With stars and moss
Had choices
With the laws.

LEAVING

Leaving is like dying a bit,
Then, arriving is what?
Getting born a bit?
Leaving is like dying a bit,
Then, I died when mother had me,
When she passed me through,
When to this world I arrived,
Leaving is like dying a bit,
Then little by little, I kept dying
When I was born
'Cause when you leave a place
You arrive somewhere and change face
I am a bit tired of this unstoppable game
Of this idiotic game that starts by ending,
That starts to end,
Of this toy that I am, and of the odious game
That spins my life around
Leaving is like dying a bit
And dying is leaving without tail
It's leaving for the end
Of all the weekends,
Going straight, going softly
But going where?
I prefer a place without mysteries,
Even if it's full of problems,
For the moment I remain here.

MY DAUGHTER'S GONNA DRIVE

My daughter's gonna drive a car
Oh, well, I said no,
I said no
Until today.

My daughter grabbing the steering wheel
Makes me lose the common sense
For whatever technical,
Because I think at her life.

My daughter acting as a driver,
I am so afraid
That I brake hard
With my thoughts
When I take her
To the exam.

My daughter drove me
On her own,
Yes, I am so proud
But I cannot cheer
If this iron cart
Isn't paid too smart
That is, much too dear.

MY DAUGHTER IN EUROPE

One April day, my sweet and shy daughter
Fluttering incessantly her wings
Left for Europe, she left to find
The air of the country of her father
The sea of her mother
And a cleaner culture
But to be somehow more sure
She left to pursue her life

She's flying away through life at nineteen
In a horizontal tour of the horizon
On our Boreal egg, and I am full of affection
But without reason envious of her.
My wife asks me if I sigh after my daughter.
What can I say? As if to order I respond,
But in my shell, my soul is moved,
I am happy and I feel how much.
Yes, I am old, she is in Europe,
I sent her with a serene air
To mix with the world,
A bit of London and some Paris,
A bit of Spain and some Italy.
Old world, she comes to ring the bell,
Greece, the sky, and Israel.

FRUCTIDOR

My wife, my good wife
Loves the flowers /The warmth
Of their colours / The charm
Of their forms/ Full of harmony
And their happy tranquility
But I know that in her soul
She loves without respite /Their promises
Of being of low maintenance
Me, I'm different / I pretend to be
A man of common sense
I like in the flowers / The smell
Of what's going to be
It's the odour / That makes me feel good
Being the announcement
Of a development.
I love the flowers / But my life
Is the fruits:
Yes, the fruits of an Apple-tree
Yes, the fruits of a Cherry-tree
Yes, the fruits of the sin
Yes, the fruit of a peach
Yes, the fruits of the Earth
Yes, the fruits of the sea
Yes, the fruits of a mother and of a father
Or of no matter what pair
Yes, the fruits of my passion
Yes, the fruits of my reason
I love the fruits
Because they contain
The principle, the source, the grains,
The germs themselves of life.

LOVE IS BIZARRE

Love is bizarre
I swear
A heart vibration
Sudden desire
For the near one
Dear need for the flesh
To see the view
Of a cheek
The image of your own
Crazy and king soul
In the soul of another
Pity
Love is a mirage
But what happens
Always
In that love
In the true love
What takes shape
Is the subtlety of change
Of a personal person
Selfish and cruel
In a sublime personality
That forgets itself
That gives itself
That gives
And becomes good at heart
Or even better

The true love is bizarre
I swear
What a pity that all that love
Is always like a montage,
A mirage

INFINITY

Under the blue skies,
Depending where you are,
Clouds cover or they bar
The view of your eyes.
That's why sometimes
One can't see
Infinity.

INQUIRY

What 's wrong with me? If I dare to say
What others don't dare, if I dare to write
What others avoid, if I dare to do
What others, terrified, shun, what's left to think
What others think, sometimes about me, but mostly
What's left to think about the thoughts of the world
That lives like on a different planet,
That drives like crazy consuming its breath,
That pleases itself with the gadgets of nonsense,
That cares about oneself without limit,
That brings itself to the brink of the cliff,
Painting a rainbow for the colour of doom.

SCANT STORY

Since the mists of time have spread
Now with heat, now with ice dread,
Huge play is played in a breath
For a life or for a death.
Pause is not in time and space,
Just a harsh flow in a race
That it happens with a whirl
And from gas, stars will unfurl
Stuffing dots in the deep night
Till they turn to rocks of light,
Smoothed as globes that keep their turn
Acting planets in hot burn,
Where magma boils, then cools,
Clearing drops in ocean pools,
Spreading waves with their hard knocks
Over sea sides, breaking rocks
That make alcoves, narrow threads,
Shape lives that swarm on their beds,
Just passing as life so goes,
Brings birth, sighs, then out it blows,
Leaving place, juice, energy
For some other entity
In a flow of changes that seem to rejoice
For the matter's progress to exert its choice,
So the planet reaches its vastness of riches
And instils the thinking for apes up to witches,
And the poet launches thought to thought in flight
His scant story towards those who take his plight.

EINSTEIN

Einstein looked at us amused
And being such a lover of people
Has thought to offer a key
For the truth to all the faces
For all the time, for all the space:
The space moves around the matter
Which bends at its turn the space,
Matter and energy are the same thing
In the right amount, if you multiply the matter
With the speed of light at the second power,
The light holds up in the Universe
Its priority of velocity,
The flow of time, very grave thing,
Depends of gravity itself
Because of the matter's amount
And that gravity is
In inverse ratio to the squared distance
Between two bodies
In the Universe everything is relative
But the laws of nature certainly
Are the same both in the large
As well as in the small infinity
In the Universe of ourselves
The same laws rule.

MY WALLS

All things, all beings
No matter what
Must pass in time
And in their space
Each things has an amount
It seems to have a territory
Delimited, well restricted
And walled up

But me, I think
I am not limited at all
I am not restricted
My walls, gilded and twisted,
Of Doric order, can be found
In the garbage of physics
Greyish network, sample
Of all the four dimensions
My walls are soft
And full of holes
My walls are found a night
In the black holes
And the next moment
In the soul of a Gioconde
That's to say in the small
Or in the large infinity
My walls whisper:
I want to mature

2708 WHAT IS THE MEANING
Music & lyrics ©Laurian Taler, 2013

A1
Why do we ask always
In this unknown life maze
What is the meaning of love
What is the meaning of love
Is it a mixture of feelings
With the attraction to one
As I want you so much
Or is it just
The huge self-love that I hide
Within a play that might work
Left inside me
From games of survival
That some ancestors played
I recognize it is not very savvy
To ask about love

A2
Instead of asking of
Words that are so deep, like
What is the meaning of love
What is the meaning of love
We should hold hands and together
Soak up of each other's gaze
Until souls are ablaze
Then dance embraced
As the birds of the sky
Before they build their nest
And change the moments
That make us happy
In timeless desire
To break the code of the powerful meaning
The answer to love

INDECENCY

Indecency grew shameless
Dancing frenetic, aimless,
Freedom to counter-balance,
Stamping deep its own valence
In chaos and disorder
Unframed by any border,

We saw the realm of thrashers
Pretending to be smashers
Of rules and laws of nature,
Not knowing what they wager

From fun with masks and ghosts,
From bullying to boasts,
From usurping cadavers
To become zombie lovers,

The new etiquette rulers,
Never of goodness poolers,
Stand up, ask for attention,
For decency's suspension,
Ready with smirk to butcher
A generation's future.

PROSETRY

What the hell is going on
With the shmart of prosetry,
Where has the beauty gone,
Maybe in the toiletry?
When you try to read some verse
That a prosem claims to be
It appears as a curse
'Cause just prose you feel and see
That's why prosets I shall call
Those that killed the rhythm and rhyme,
Who with verses play bad ball
Mixing logorrhoea slime
With the nonsense of savants
Of the belles-lettristic type
Making prosems into rants
And creating only tripe.

HAPPY TO KNOW

I am happy to know
That the wind that will blow
Will inflate well your sails
And no matter if gales
You encounter, you'll find
Powers, moods of all kind
To arrive at your ports
With the wisdom of sorts
That you'll learn to achieve
While your dreams you will weave.

94 SNOWGRASS

Music & lyrics ©Laurian Taler, 2007, 2011

A1
Snowgrass makes me think of you
Thin, green, and so tough to handle
On the mountains of my youth
Seeking a higher truth

A2
Snowgrass brings back memories
Of the time that we were younger
When we went to see the world
And in the grass we curled

B
Our sky was bluer
The horizon larger
The valleys deeper
Our eyes brighter
And we flew farther
Wings of desire
That flapped as our hearts
Sang the beauty surrounding, oh

Our sky was bluer
The horizon larger
The valleys deeper
Our eyes brighter
And we flew farther
Wings of desire
That flapped as our hearts
Sang the beauty surrounding our love

FUN

fun
is having your eyes
full of sun
it is acting wise
and seeing yourself
not more than an elf
or a speck of dust
if you really must
measure up in a curse
with the whole Universe

fun
is laughing out loud
under a cloud
of uncertainties
or maybe it is
crying, crying, crying after
another good laughter

fun
is getting a run
to crushing the bone
from whomever's throne
it's singing the praise
of whatever good craze
that makes human the beast
that used so much its fist
to rule over the crowd;
fun is to be proud
that you put up the mettle
with ugly not to settle
and you act within danger
to become a world changer
'cause it's not too much fun
without eyes full of sun

FIFTY-TWO

When suddenly, you get to fifty-two,
The doubts get deep and soul is asking, "Who
Are you, a twenty-fiver, if you reverse the sight,
Or twenty-six if on one leg you fight?"

Along, you gather wonders of a tale
And if your limbs are stretched to right a sail
You thumb your nose at age and hide it well.
Who's under times? It's facts that play the spell.

What if the bone again screams silent aches
Under the iron bloodied by tough life,
What follows a shield always makes
And mind arrives to conquer strife.

You round yourself with grace and wit,
Horizons watch and see what's full
And sniff the air out of pit
With charm the poison's sweeten cool,

You party, dream, and still party again,
But idly wait the elevator's cling
To lift you up to what just work can bring
And make your flight a one that's truly sane.

39A I WISH I COULD

Music & lyrics ©Laurian Taler, 2000

I wish I could turn back the time
To when father held me on his neck
I wish I could turn back the time
So that I could give him what he'd missed
(bis)

2
A walk to park, a play with stones
And a little song, a throw of cones
A secret handshake, two kind words
So that I could give him what he'd missed
(bis)

3
War just took him
Like a tree leaf
And then dropped him
In its whirl
Lands and people
Kept him long time
As an oyster keeps its pearl
And he suffered in his slavery
And we suffered 'cause his bravery
When he came back
I was too old to be carried
On his back
I forgot the games he taught me
And he had to find his track

Sagacity

A walk to park, a play with stones
And a little song, a throw of cones
A secret handshake, two kind words
So that I could give him what he'd missed
(bis)

I wish I could turn back the time
To when father held me on his neck
I wish I could turn back the time
So that I could give him what he'd missed
(bis)

63   A POETS' SONG

Music & lyrics © Laurian Taler, 2001

A
Words are only tools we sculpt with
Into what some say is soul
Probing and disrobing whole
What is sadness or is bliss

Sounds of thoughts we craft to see
Into lines of song and pain
Trying to make sense in vain
Of what life is or should be

B
Proud words we spread down
To chant and enchant - (as poets)
Humble we hope that
We write what we meant - (as poets)

Strings of our feelings
We try soft to twinge
Playing with words means
We sing and we singe

54 WAKE UP

Music & lyrics ©Laurian Taler, 2000

1
Wake up 'cause
Dreams are running nowhere
Dreams are running a - nowhere
You ought to
Wake for action, act out, dreamer
Time goes by if you don't simmer
(bis)
Dreams are running only if you act

2
Go out, find your way around,
Go and make it with your sound,
Go and claim your right to be
As you have dreamed

Do your best and try again,
Don't be sleepy, don't be vain,
Serve your sisters, build a place,
Be full of grace

Count the seconds doing good,
Waste no time in a bad mood,
Live the present, face the future,
Wake up

2803 ECHO OF YOUTH

Music & lyrics ©Laurian Taler, 2014

A1
The sounds of other time
And the songs full of sweet rhyme
In the fields where we walked
Holding hands while we talked
Kisses in the woods that gave us shade
All your laughs and your smiles for me

A2
The sky bluer than blue
The horizons without clue
And the passion that so grew
For a life, right and true
Kisses in the woods that gave us shade
All your laughs and your smiles for me

B (2x)
With the echo of my youth vibrating
With the echo of my youth alive
Glimpses of our strive
In my mind revive
What was for both
Fascinating time

PHONETIC ETHICS

Today we'll work
On a sound
The air wave
That carries the mysteries
The fantastic noise
Transformed in music
The tremor of the earth
Which becomes word
The enchanted of the phrase
That takes us to ecstasy
The unfailing tone
That makes itself sermon
A sound in sequence
That makes us march in cadence
Word-play sometimes searing
That slips into swearing
But what really counts
It's not just the sound from the mounds
It is how it's tied
It's not just the word
But its role
It's not the many words
It's their connections
If a sound is a detail of science
The importance is in the conscience
What counts, I hear myself mumble,
It is not the detail, it is the ensemble.

2403 LOST SAIL

Music & lyrics ©Laurian Taler, 2014

A1
Rowing on some turbulent waves
We may reach islands with graves and raves
Rowing when smooth and when in a gale
We feel like we have lost sail

A2
Life's a dance on the up and the down
Carry your jacket as not to drown
Make sure you have with what to out-bail
Even if you lost your sail

B (2x)
Hold tight, the waves will calm,
Hold tight, life's in your palms,
Hold tight at any cost
With hope you are never lost

A1, A2, B (2x)

DECIMAL SYSTEM

One day the poet
Had to count his loves
Much as you count your socks or gloves
He had to count by heart
How many hearts,
By good work or mistake
Was he able to take.

The list wasn't long or short
'Cause never wrote how he cavort
By this I say that he did mount
But he forgot his loves to count

That's not only to say
That he forgot to count
The units, zlot by zlot,
It is the digits he forgot

The digits, yes, the figures,
The Arab ones, also the Romans
All of a sudden, he realized
He could count zilch

He had so long used just words
Always just words
With their qualities,
With their strange gearing
That never the quantities
In the language for him
Became decoded, and you see, so
The digits vanished from his memory

So then, to quantify the truth
And to be on his way

Of counting his list
The poet had to imagine
A decimal system
Without digits, without nulls
But made of words
More or less normal

Words measure, words of fire
Words of honour, of desire,
That was not that easy
But he got really busy
Finding satisfaction
With the words of action

Being
  Receiving
    Acting
  Knowing
Measuring
  Understanding
    Developing
  Sharing
Loving
  Creating

His decimal system
Of words not too bad
Were turning in mind
As spiralled to his head

Here is my philosophy,
Said he to himself,
Not bad what I made
From a list of whom I laid.

FROM THE EARTH

From the earth I took, with care
Just a hand grey made of clay
To fashion a jug with flair
Only-I filled it with green whey
From the finest brook I swallowed
Crystal water that came down
But I couldn't quench the fire
Even with amounts to drown
From the sun I caught a light beam
With its warmth to make more straight
My mind, not exactly up-stream
And my sigh and my poor gait
From the wind I sucked in breathing
That passes over this land
And my songs I got releasing
Made of words and sounds of band
From my friends, who with their talking
Told me wise thoughts from a sage
Where is heaven I kept knocking
On the stairs, growing age
Around parents, sister, brother
I built shield full of emotions
And deposed a coin to smother
With truth all kinds of demotions
Only Time, which moments greases
In long fractions made of doom
Gathers me, turns me to pieces
When to win I closer zoom

THE FLAT POETRY

I was born with tongue in cheek
But words in ten tongues I seek
So that I can read the riddles
Even written with code fiddles
That's why I try to avoid
Blessing or cursing in void
When I meet the lines of words
That seemed made only for birds
Shabby bills, price undefined
That the readers mind they grind
Neither fixers nor translators
Find meaning from the "creators"
- No balm for flat poetry
Can fix flatters' coterie
Sudden march from bad to worse
Of the flat, flat, flat, flat verse
So that you may ask how come
It keeps jumping and then some
From angels from sky deposed
To non-sense completely closed
For those considered low class
Who some rhymes prefer to pass
And with all the poems features
And meaning for rowdy creatures.
This is why I wonder, why,
Is the poet blunt or dry
That he doesn't see the gap
Between prose and his own sap
Or his grey matter went bad
And is recognized as mad
That, being blind as a bat,
Doesn't see he's poet flat.

THESE KIDS

Oh, how these kids have grown
With their saintly glow
We watch them now, and as were known
Savouring the past and throe
They leave, and we us both remain
To cry over their photo grain.
They sweetened our love these kids
And lengthened our sensual skids
Have made us better, dried us up
Have squeezed all out of our sup,
What did for them was done so deep
Now what we've sown, we maybe reap
Their glare caresses our soul
They glow and we have reached our goal.

WE FIND OURSELVES

We always find ourselves on path
When at a ford, when at a crossing
Smoke' s on sky, in us with wrath
The way we don't know where is tossing
With no signs, and maps amiss
Guides are lost in the abyss
We keep on pacing in small round
Choosing when a glen, when mound
Pushing coffin, pushing shield
But our soul is hardly healed
Quarrelling like anyone
Knowing nought under the sun
The way 's narrow and is thorny
We get proud and we get corny
On our fragile and thin legs
Arguing that our dregs
Take us to a side of way
But we keep on anyway
Teeming in our souls the faith
Coming from an untrue wraith
Till we turn to smoke or clay.
We find ourselves.

MY DAUGHTER

My daughter with a sage's name
In grievous crossing arms on chest
Directs herself at looking an invisible ray
And hopes with patient stare,
And mute it is her say
Sliding with leisure that rounds her in her game
She gathers rest in her jaws,
The moves are killed at best
She enters with her pacing
A world of empty nests
And pain and ache evoking,
Creates film with ghost guests
Throwing herself in vortex
She whispers verse of light
She floats over the waters
And flies slow through the night
Dislodges with her gaze
Tall shades hidden in mountains
And brings out light from maze
On foreheads arched on fountains
Tying now with tomorrow, sensing the past in air
Fight, kiss and love conceiving
Removing a small glare
Of frights and of unknown
She dances densely her life
As she has thought and sewn

TILES

Tiles, tiles, more tiles, tiles, tiles, more tiles,
Trivets, pots, potters' creations
My daughter paints massive clay plates
Tiles and pots with decorations
When she colours and shapes lays
We in wonder gaze through glaze
My daughter is painting fruits
On the dirt that's burnt by sun
Fruits more soft than bamboo shoots
Oh! My heart feels as if stun!
My daughter paints butterflies,
Small and big fish, and blue skies
Paints the dark and paints the sunshine
And the dawn and dusk with blood line
My daughter paints two sweet angels
On trivets she draws the saints
And the forest with restraints,
Taking out the shades from paints
My daughter draws lively nudes
And paints cities in decay
With three lines she changes moods
Of her soul she makes display
Tiles and pots and decorations
Shields and fields and light of air
From the earth she lays them bare
With her brushes' applications
Who will look and weigh her glazed tiles
Who will eat from painted jugs
Who will drink from her sweet mugs
Who will look at them with shrugs
Or will ask what hugger-mugger
Brought them out toward art's plugger
To warm up the wistful souls
Tiles and trivets, mugs and pots
For the haves and for have-nots

PAPER ANGELS

Cutting out some paper angels
That would jump out of a book
Comes out also ardent question
But the answer 's hard to look
Why in good guard many beings
Try to cover with some saints
When they don't see what faith can do
And don't understand constraints
Why their faith they cheat so easy
Looking up to sky and paints
When the sky empty 's of saints
Why in loneliness of certain
Human flesh deludes in night
And afraid of its mind curtains
Hunching prays, throws out its bite
Toward nothingness of light
Passionately spells up god names
Trembling low in the sunset
And at wonders dreams and claims
Why when bad luck sometimes shows up
Its hard flesh frets of a sudden
From ghost, son and then from father
Squeezing sacred guardianship
When truth is lords and saints and gods
Are being built in the night hour
And cheat themselves in their pacts
Who in ghosts believe, and not in facts

ONLY POETS AND SOME MADMEN

Only poets and some madmen
Have found out what real love is
Eggheads, scientists or wise men
Found out just what is oblivion

Dying souls feel with their heart full
But the mind plays them bizarre
Life with speed flows out bountiful
Choosing now heaven, now tar,
Squirming with so much so pride
And in lust more long than wide,
Looking for unreachable skies
And horizons without end
From the life that was at bend
Toward a life that's beyond,
They pay with precious grey matter
Hopelessness they don't abscond
And they crawl with their treasures
Digesting in them old pleasures

Only poets and some madmen,
Souls that held themselves at bay,
Have found out what real love is
And have lived for love to weigh

Come to me, you, my mad soul,
Oblivion I shall console

JOYFUL SIGH

When I with sandals walk
To head I get a shock,
If a shoe hurts my leg
A sigh from heart I dreg
And if the boot 's too small
My pubis I enthral
And 'cause I 'm like a sloth
Of ageing I am loath
But I with sneakers care
Half century to wear,
A virgin I don't look,
Don't use gobbledygook
'Cause I am proud of all,
My feet being so small
And honours folks bestow
To make me sigh and glow

WHAT HURT YOU

What hurt you more
Wasn't that the flame didn't kindle
Under my such tumultuous breath
What hurt you more indeed it was
That tear drop didn't flow out
From secret happiness at dawn
When, opening lights out of sky,
You could have brought yourself neat down
To a tender vagrant soul,
'T wasn't enough I offered you
What you refused as worldly grace
T' wasn't enough to worship you
With smouldering embers, watching clue
To eyes so deep and soft and blue
You wanted me strait-laced and set,
It wouldn't do what lovers get,
Knowing what you lose and feeling so wise
Looking straight, quite scared in my green eyes
You've chosen the chill of the mind
Against the heat of flesh and kind,
When time just of moments is made
You let it grow and then to fade,
The love's unpaid and sweet tribute
Has overwhelmed you and it hurt
And you preferred to-avoid the aches
But life that doesn't meet the hurt
Flattens down a real being
What hurt you most was just your calm
That I've taken apart
And me missing at dawn in bed
And my caress that so you lost
Ah, loneliness has made you frost

THE MERRIMENT

I gobble lives on film stock
In two hours ending with the artists
And drink the heavy liquid of the art
Rubbing elbows with important people
I read the news from cover to cover
And wonder where is the story
With gingerbread and wild mushroom
Press buttons, empty vials
And find my peace in concentrations
But romantism became now naked
I dress it up with equations
However, when debating life trends
I remember the beat of my heart
A beat that gathered the learnings
Of trotting over half a century
And then I smile to sun, to flowers
To those friends that hum with me
And laugh at crying, in pain crying
But merriment is still much grander
Than space and than eternity

YOU WANTED TOO MUCH

You wanted too much
My handcuffs caught
In your flesh
My suitcase pushed
Under your bed
And the tie that I don't wear
Tied gingerly by you
Every morning
You wanted too much
Your hand reaching
Under the white quilt
Toward my shoulder
To avert the scare of emptiness
The morning coffee
Taken with understandings
In the eyes
And the noise of the bathroom
As is made by the one who
Really lives there
Listened to with
Drunken wonder by you
What you didn't want to accept
Was all these unwound
In the coil of the mind
And that warm look
Turned toward the stone
Of your conscience
Look that was coming and coming
And would have been enough
For a second eternity.

WHAT KIND OF TREMOR

What kind of tremor goes through the eye-shadows
When you show up as if from the waves
Of rays you take shape, and of foam
Friend, lover, spouse, mother
What kind of tremor do I feel in my lips
When you smile to me and I see muses
That invite me to sing your fine features
And to kiss your hand and your saint footprint
What kind of waves go through my skin
When you try me in every way
And when you gather me in your arms
I melt, I know what greed is
What kind of waves break with a noise
When you are looking into my soul
And you surround me with your pride
Friend, lover, spouse, mother and bride
What kind of flutters go through my blood
When you hold tight and my heart also tightens
Of such an infinity that I feel again like a groom
What kind of flames in me are burning
When you make time in emptiness to lose itself
And the moments of longing
To seem to stay for ever
Friend, spouse, mother and again my lover.

1308 HOLD TIGHT ON THE RIDE

Music & lyrics ©Laurian Taler, 2005

A1
Hold tight on the ride
It's up and down
Hold tight on the ride
It's like a tide
Hold tight on the ride
You cannot hide
Bring out your emotions
Or you'll die
A2
Hold tight on the ride
I am your guide
Hold tight on the ride
Don't eat your pride
Hold tight on the ride
The turns are wide
Bring out your emotions
Be a clown
B1
Life is us riding together,
In the unknown of mankind
No matter if a stormy weather
Tries to give us a hard time
B2
Life is us riding so together,
Eyes to eyes and hand in hand
With blue skies or stormy weather
Our love's a magic wand

A1

Sagacity

C
Everybody goes through life on waves
Rowing up and down
Everybody goes through life on waves
On tides
Hard as your life is
You keep afloat
With your head
Up, up in the sun
Eyes burning

A1

B1
Life is us riding together,
In the unknown of mankind
No matter if a stormy weather
Tries to give us a hard time

B3
Life is us riding together, together
Eyes to eyes and hand in hand
With blue skies or stormy weather
Our love's a magic wand
Our great love (3x)

BIO

I was born in Brasov, Romania, in 1940.
In 1952 I had a poem published in "Scanteia pionierului",
a national newspaper for children. Other poems were lost over the
years in the emigration. I started playing the clarinet and the
saxophone in high school and continued in University.
I studied Biology at Iasi University between 1959 and 1964, after
which I worked as a teacher in two high schools. Between 1969 and
1975 I published science articles as a free-launch journalist in
several newspapers and magazines, among them "Astra" and
"Romania Literara".
In 1976 I emigrated to Italy, then to Canada in 1978, where I
worked initially in biochemistry, then in Toronto schools.
In 1997 I started writing songs and lyrics for these songs.
Several of these songs have been released in two compact disks and
online.
In 2007 I wrote the environmental musical "One Earth".
In 2013 I published several e-books online with Amazon.
At this time I prepare the publication of several books,
some of lyrics and poetry, some of prose, within my own publishing
company, Gong Publishing.

SAGACITY
POEMS

©Laurian Taler

GONG PUBLISHING
TORONTO

www.gongnog.com

ISBN 978-1-926477-01-5

www.ingramcontent.com/pod-product-compliance
Lightning Source LLC
Chambersburg PA
CBHW071110090426
42737CB00013B/2554